TRA JP

D1556732

LONDON MIDLAND STEAM: Skipton-Carlisle

LONDON MIDLAND STEAM
STEAM
SKIPTON - CARLISLE

R. H. LESLIE and **R. H. SHORT**

D. BRADFORD BARTON LIMITED

Frontispiece: The 'Thames-Clyde Express' running between London (St. Pancras) and Glasgow (St. Enoch) was the principal express passenger train over the Settle-Carlisle line. Rebuilt 'Royal Scot' No. 46145 *The Duke of Wellington's Regt. (West Riding)*, a class which was the mainstay of heavy passenger train work during the last twenty years of steam operation, forges up the climb out of Carlisle towards Cotehill with the southbound train on 26 June 1960.

© copyright D. Bradford Barton 1976   *ISBN 0 85153 223 3*

printed in Great Britain by H. E. Warne Ltd, London and St. Austell

for the publishers

D. BRADFORD BARTON LTD · Trethellan House . Truro . Cornwall · England

introduction

A century ago, the 73-mile long main line through the very heart of the Pennines from Settle to Carlisle was within measurable sight of completion, an epic achievement of railway construction in Britain. This line had the distinction of being the last trunk route to be constructed almost entirely by traditional methods, and since early in 1870 the navvies—at times numbering over 6,000—battled against a remote, inhospitable terrain and appalling winter weather conditions, labouring with nothing save their muscles and simple tools, excavating hundreds of thousands of tons of rock, boulder clay and earth. Major works like Blea Moor Tunnel, and the massive viaducts at Ribblehead, Dent Head, Arten Gill and Smardale each took four to five years to construct.

Against every conceivable setback, the determination of the Midland Railway Company and the contractors won through; freight trains were using the line from the summer of 1875 and the first passenger train ran on 1 May 1876.

The background to this prodigious venture was typical of Victorian railway politics. The ambitious Midland Railway, having reached Lancaster and Ingleton over the metals of the North Western Railway—the 'little' North Western—opened throughout from Skipton in 1849, cast envious eyes upon the lucrative and rapidly increasing Anglo-Scottish traffic, but attempts to gain a share by running through carriages and freight over the Ingleton-Low Gill line, thence to Carlisle, were discouraged by the uncooperative attitude of the London & North Western, the Midland Company's deadly rival. So the Midland decided to seek its own route north, and successfully received Royal Assent from the House of Lords.

However, the L.N.W.R. thereupon decided that co-operation was preferable to competition and the two companies eventually agreed upon joint operation of the Lancaster & Carlisle line if the Midland would apply for an Abandonment Bill for its own line. This was done, but Parliament, becoming rather tired of speculative railway schemes, turned down the Bill. The new line must be built.

There were no half-measures about the route chosen. The young Tasmanian engineer, John Sharland, skilfully surveyed an alignment which, despite the difficult nature of the country, resulted in a main line to the highest standards. With one exception, there were no speed restrictions to less than 70 m.p.h. and the ruling gradient was kept at a maximum of 1 in 100.

The route passes through some of the most beautiful scenery in England. From Skipton in the heart of the pleasant Craven country, the line climbs gradually to a summit just south of Hellifield then descends to the Ribble Valley at Settle Junction where the Lancaster line swings away to the north-west. From the junction, the new line begins the continuous ascent of Ribblesdale—up what is termed 'The Long Drag'—to Blea Moor Tunnel. Emerging from the tunnel, the line, now well above the 1000ft contour, is carried high on the hillside, giving a superb view of Dentdale far below. At Garsdale, the line turns due north again and reaches Ais Gill signal box, at 1169ft above sea level the highest main line summit in England. Thereafter the line descends along the side of the Mallerstang valley in company with the infant River Eden, which remains close at hand for the rest of the journey to Carlisle. The scenery on the final stretch between Appleby and Carlisle is in parts the most beautiful on the whole line.

Against this dramatic and magnificent landscape, the steam locomotive was in its element. Whether battling against the long, hard gradients under the shadow of great hills like Ingleborough, Whernside and Wild Boar Fell, or speeding along Dentdale and the Eden Valley, it was the perfect setting for this most fascinating of machines.

R. H. Leslie contributed the first part of the volume, from Carlisle to Garsdale, and R. H. Short the second part from Garsdale south to Skipton.

Stanier's three-cylinder 'Jubilee' 4-6-0s performed regular passenger work on the Settle-Carlisle line for over 25 years. No. 45715 *Invincible* faces the long, hard pull to Ais Gill Summit as she leaves Citadel Station at Carlisle with the 9.50 a.m. (SO) Edinburgh (Waverley)-Nottingham express on 29 July 1961.

The Settle-Carlisle line diverges from the Carlisle-Newcastle route at Petteril Bridge Junction, seen here in the background, and runs alongside to Durranhill Junction. At the latter, 'Jubilee' No. 45597 *Barbados* restarts a Kingmoor-Kings Norton van train from a signal stop on 23 March 1963.

The 1.04 p.m. Carlisle-Skipton freight invariably conveyed a fascinating assortment of vehicles and loads. 'Crab' 2-6-0 No. 42831 heads south past Scotby with this train on 16 February 1964.

The 'Patriot' Class 4-6-0s appeared regularly on express passenger workings over the Settle-Carlisle line in the 1930s when new. In post-war years, however, they were rare visitors to the line and it was unusual to see No. 45502 *Royal Naval Division* heading a northbound relief near Cotehill on 28 December 1957.

The up 'Thames-Clyde Express' hauled by rebuilt 'Royal Scot' No. 46113 *Cameronian* passing throug Cumwhinton, 10 June 1956. Cumwhinton, a typical example of the neatly laid out stations on the S & was closed five months after the date of this photograph. The remaining intermediate stations north Settle, with the exception of Appleby, were closed and local services withdrawn on 5 May 1970.

The magnificent BR Standard 9F Class 2-10-0s worked on the S & C from the late 1950s right to the end of steam. In 1959, three of these locomotives were fitted with mechanical stokers and allocated to Saltley shed for working accelerated freights between Washwood Heath and Carlisle. No. 92167, so equipped, thunders up the climb past the site of Cotehill station with the 4.13 p.m. Durranhill-Washwood Heath on 18 August 1959.

the summer of 1957, daytime trains between Edinburgh and London (St. Pancras) were given the happy le of 'The Waverley', after the popular name of the route between Carlisle and Edinburgh. 'Britannia' acific No. 70054 *Dornoch Firth* storms up the 1 in 132 climb near Cotehill with the 10.05 a.m. from Edinburgh, March 1961.

The characteristic sharp exhaust beat of a Caprotti Class 5 4-6-0 echoes over the Cumbrian countryside as No. 44754 heads an up evening freight on 1 May 1958 over High Stand Viaduct at Cotehill.

Looking smart in shiny black paint, Class 4F 0-6-0 No. 44055 newly out of works, climbs briskly past Cotehill with a southbound freight from Durranhill, 19 November 1960.

14

The summit of the initial eight-mile climb out of Carlisle is reached at the south end of the deep cutting before Low House Crossing. Midland Railway 4F 0-6-0 No. 44007 hauls a southbound freight over the top on 3 May 1958. Something like another 25 miles of undulating sections follow before the main climb begins to Ais Gill.

'Crab' 2-6-0 No. 42882 tops the summit with steam shut off, Low House distant signal being at caution, a result of the crossing gates not having been closed to road traffic quite early enough, 3 May 1958.

South of the summit, the line follows the valley of the beautiful River Eden closely for the next fifteen mile or so. With a patchwork of Pennine farmsteads in the distance, 'Britannia' Class No.70044 *Earl Haig* sweeps up the 1 in 132 gradient past Low House with the 10.35 a.m. Leeds-Glasgow on 9 April 1960.

With steam already shut off for the forthcoming stop at Armathwaite, Class 4 2-6-0 No.43004 gallops down towards Dry Beck Viaduct with the 6.05 p.m. Carlisle-Appleby local on 29 July 1963. Next to the engine are two empty milk tanks for the Express Dairies depot at Appleby.

e signalman at Low House watches the passage of the down 'Thames-Clyde Express' making short rk of the gradient behind rebuilt 'Royal Scot' No. 46112 *Sherwood Forester* on 18 August 1959.

anier Class 8F 2-8-0 No. 48399 accelerates a southbound express freight down past Low House Crossing 18 August 1959, working up a good speed which will be maintained over the easily-graded stretch of e towards the crossing of the River Eden beyond Lazonby.

The fireman of Class 5 4-6-0 No. 44852 takes a brief rest from his labours as his engine thunders through Armathwaite station at the head of an express freight from Carlisle to the Midlands on a May evening in 1960.

BR Standard Class 5
No. 73122 speeds
through Armathwaite
with an Edinburgh
(Waverley)-Nottingham
express on 20 July
1957.

The 11.35 a.m.
Hellifield-Carlisle local
is restarted from
Armathwaite, the last
stop before Carlisle,
by 'Jubilee' No. 45697
Achilles on 20 July
1957. The station here
is sited on a hillside
high above the
village.

The elegant Fowler 2-6-4Ts frequently worked the local trains over the S & C in the early 1960s. No. 42313, smartly turned out by Kingmoor shed, pulls away from the attractively-situated station at Armathwaite with the 6.05 p.m. Carlisle-Appleby, 5 June 1962.

22

The down 'Thames-Clyde Express' hauled by rebuilt 'Royal Scot' No. 46145 *The Duke of Wellington's Regt.* (*West Riding*), in beautiful Eden Valley surroundings at Armathwaite Viaduct, 10 June 1956.

The Settle-Carlisle line is noted for its fine viaducts and although the most spectacular of these are to be found on the mountain section there are many other impressive memorials to the skill of the stone-masons of a century ago, like Armathwaite, 176 yards long, 80 feet high, fashioned in local red sandstone and blending in well with the local scenery. Class 5 No. 44672 crosses with a southbound van train on 28 April 1967.

24

Well-kept No. 44584, one of the Fowler 4F 0-6-0s which rendered yeoman service on the line for something like fifty years, gleams in the autumn sunshine as she heads a Carlisle-Leeds freight round the long curve leading to Armathwaite Tunnel on 19 October 1957.

'Jubilee' No. 45707 *Valiant* speeds along the lovely stretch of line at Baron Wood, approaching Armathwaite, with the **9.25 a.m. SO** London (St. Pancras)-Glasgow (St. Enoch) express on 20 August 1960.

The rugged, ungainly LMS Class 5 2-6-0s, known as 'Crabs', also performed sterling freight work over the line for 35 years; No. 42834 crossing Armathwaite Viaduct with a southbound goods from Carlisle, 27 January 1962.

Armathwaite Tunnel, 325 yards long, is the first of many on the run south from Carlisle. 'Jubilee' No. 45564 *New South Wales* has just emerged with the up 'Waverley', 28 May 1960.

Stanier Class 5 No. 44824, hauling a southbound train of tank wagons, is approaching the first of the two short Baron Wood Tunnels, 28 May 1960. Above the engine can be seen Armathwaite Viaduct, one mile distant.

'Jubilee' No. 45589 *Gwalior* heads the 10.05 a.m. Edinburgh (Waverley)-London (St. Pancras) express on the descending stretch of a mile or so at 1 in 165 approaching Lazonby, 28 April 1956.

The BR Standard 'Clan' Class Pacifics from Kingmoor shed were frequently used on the local trains. No. 72007 *Clan Mackintosh* drifts along between Culgaith and Langwathby with the 11.35 a.m. Hellifield-Carlisle on 7 July 1956.

The down 'Thames-Clyde Express' at speed north of Long Marton, double-headed by Class 2P 4-4-0 No. 40690 and 'Jubilee' No. 45568 *Western Australia*. The pair on this occasion were deputising for a 'Royal Scot', the usual motive power, and the 2P pilot will probably come off the train at Carlisle; 7 July 1956.

The 'Waverley' was frequently double-headed, a 'Jubilee', with a 'Black Five' as pilot, being a popular combination of locomotives. No. 45679 *Armada* and No. 44716 pulling away from Appleby with the southbound train on 20 August 1957 are passing the Express Dairies depot which formerly despatched considerable numbers of milk tank wagons to London, as the large sign proclaims. The rail connection to the depot is now removed, this traffic having ceased.

A northbound freight headed by 'Crab' 2-6-0 No.42905 having just emerged from Helm Tunnel is travelling fast on the final stretch of the descent towards Ormside on 20 May 1956. The name Helm is associated with the local phenomenon known as the Helm Wind, caused by conflicting masses of air over the Eden Valley and usually producing a long, straight, black cloud over Cross Fell.

The up 'Thames-Clyde Express' on 20 May 1956 hauled by 'Royal Scot' No. 46133 *The Green Howards* approaches Helm Tunnel on the first stage of the 1 in 100 climb from Ormside to Griseburn signal box. In the misty distance, the hills rise towards Cross Fell, the highest mountain in the Pennines.

At Griseburn, near milepost 272, the halfway point between Carlisle and Settle, the gradient becom easier for a short distance onward towards Crosby Garrett. 'Royal Scot' No. 46117 *Welsh Guardsm* topping the first stage of 1 in 100 as she crosses Griseburn Viaduct with the up 'Waverley' on 20 Augu 1960. Possibly the train brakes were dragging slightly, for No. 46117 was being worked almost to the limit maintain about 35 m.p.h. with her nine-coach load.

34

Class 4F No. 44119 passes under a high-arched bridge spanning the deep rock cutting near Crosby Garrett as she plods along with an up freight from Carlisle on 19 July 1958. The Midland Railway did not attempt to economize when it came to providing bridges and even those carrying minor roads and farm occupation tracks were substantially constructed.

A Summer Saturday Ayr-Liverpool express hauled by Class 5 No. 44669 crossing Smardale Viaduct over the deep, thickly-wooded valley of the Scandal Beck on 3 August 1957. The viaduct, at 130ft the highest on the line, also crossed the former North Eastern Railway branch from Kirkby Stephen to Tebay, now lifted, the line passing under the southernmost arch.

'Britannia' Class No. 70016 *Ariel* heads a St. Pancras-Glasgow (St. Enoch) relief express out of Birkett Tunnel, under Wharton Fell, on 22 July 1967. The tunnel here, 424 yards long, was driven through the geological feature known as the Great Pennine Fault and the varied rocks encountered caused serious problems for the engineers. Examples of the rock strata, often lying in different directions, are visible in the deep cutting at the south end.

Probably the hardest duty over the line entrusted to the Class 9F 2-10-0s was the haulage of the anhydrite trains from the British Gypsum mine at Long Meg, near Little Salkeld, to the United Sulphuric Acid Corporation works at Widnes in Lancashire. Usually made up to twenty wagons, with a trailing load of around 700 tons, these were heavy trains and the locomotives required careful handling on the part of the enginemen, especially in the bad weather conditions frequently encountered. On a fine afternoon in June 1967, however, there are no such problems as No. 92098 blasts out of Birkett Tunnel and rouses the echoes in the deep cutting as she slogs up the 1 in 100 at a steady twenty miles per hour.

A sad day for the Settle-Carlisle line and the closing of an era on Britain's railways. 11 August 1968 saw the end of steam and a feature of everyday life disappeared. To mark the occasion, British Railways ran an excursion from Liverpool to Carlisle and back, using the Settle-Carlisle line in both directions. Stanier 'Black Fives' Nos. 44871 and 44781 are on familiar ground as they double-head the returning train up the Mallerstang Valley towards Ais Gill. Here, the line is carried high on the hillside overlooking the valley and Mallerstang Edge, rising to well over 2,000'.

9F 2-10-0 No. 92205 crosses Ais Gill Viaduct at the head of the Mallerstang Valley as she makes a laborious climb towards the summit with the afternoon Long Meg-Widnes anhydrite train on a typical overcast, drizzly, Pennine day; 20 May 1967.

The Stanier Class 8F 2-8-0s were the backbone of freight motive power on the Settle-Carlisle line for many years until gradually superseded by the 9F 2-10-0s. No. 48758 blasts up towards Ais Gill with the afternoon Carlisle-Stourton freight on 25 June 1960. The train is passing the site of the tragic Ais Gill disaster of 1913 when, during darkness, a passenger train over-ran the signals at Mallerstang and collided with the rear of the preceding sleeping-car train which had stalled just a half-mile from the summit through the engine being short of steam.

A pair of 'Black Fives', Nos. 45009 and 44785, make light work of the up 'Waverley' as they charge over the final stretch of 1 in 100 to Ais Gill Summit at nearly 50 m.p.h. on 25 June 1960. The pilot engine will probably be detached at Hellifield.

'Jubilee' No. 45565 *Victoria* in classic setting against the towering bulk of Wild Boar Fell at the head of the Mallerstang Valley. On a blustery Spring day, she approaches the summit at Ais Gill with the up 'Thames-Clyde Express' on 27 March 1960.

he ageless majesty of Wild Boar Fell provides a magnificent background to the view north from Ais Gill. 8F No. 48464 ils up the last quarter-mile of 1 in 100 at little more than walking pace with an afternoon freight from Carlisle on 13 May 161. The Fell takes its name from the legend that it was reputed to be the place where the last wild boar was killed in ritain. 2,324 feet above sea level, it is one of the highest of the Pennine mountains. The top is quite flat and in clear eather there are very extensive views over many miles, especially to the north and south.

45

The 'WD' Class 2-8-0s were a wartime design for the Ministry of Supply. Rugged and functional, they appeared frequently on the line, especially towards the end of steam. No. 90012 passes Ais Gill with the 1.04 p.m. Carlisle-Skipton freight on 13 May 1961.

Despite something approaching fifteen hard miles at 1 in 100, Fowler 'Crab' No.42823 climbs strongly over the last few yards to Ais Gill summit with empty car-flats on 26 June 1960.

Ais Gill summit, 1,169 feet above sea level and the highest main-line summit in England. 'Britannia' No. 70054 *Dornoch Firth* speeds past the lonely little signal box and begins the fast downhill run to Ormside and Carlisle with the 'Waverley' on 13 May 1961.

A 'Jubilee' on the 'Waverley' looked just right! No. 45562 *Alberta* forges over the summit at Ais Gill with the up express on 13 May 1961. Steam haulage of the express passenger trains ended in the summer of 1961 although continuing on the Summer Saturday and special trains. No. 45562 from Holbeck shed at Leeds was destined to become one of the last survivors of the class when steam working over the line ceased in 1967.

'Royal Scot' No. 46145 *The Duke of Wellington's Regt. (West Riding)* heads the 9.25 a.m. (SO) London (St. Pancras) Glasgow (St. Enoch) express over Moorcock Viaduct, Garsdale, on 25 June 1960. The formation of the branch to Haw and Northallerton, closed in 1959, can be seen on the hillside in the background.

Also amongst the remaining 'Jubilee' 4-6-0s was No. 45593 *Kolhapur*. In this view, she is approaching Shotlock Hill Tunnel between Garsdale and Ais Gill, with the Saturday relief train from London (St. Pancras) to Glasgow (St. Enoch) on 12 August 1967.

North of Blea Moor Tunnel the line is carried high on the hillside overlooking Dentdale. Class 5 No. 45331 takes the curve through Dent station with a limestone train from Horton-in-Ribblesdale in September 1967. The remains of the snow-fences can be seen on the fell above the train, and on the right of the photograph is Arten Gill Viaduct.

[Peter J. Robinson]

A northbound freight headed by No. 45252 crossing Arten Gill Viaduct in October 1967. [S. C. Crook]

2-6-0 No. 42876 emerges from the southern portal of Blea Moor tunnel with a Carlisle-Skipton freight in June 1959. The tunnel, 2,629 yards long, carries the line through the mountain 500′ below the surface of the moor. The cost of construction in 1875 was £45 per yard, and many human lives.

Driver Wardman of Hellifield poses with his charge, No.42834, whilst the locomotive is watered at Bl Moor loops, and the fireman views the scene from atop the tender.

Leaving Blea Moor loops, the tracks run northwards in a straight line through the approach cutting to Blea Moor Tunnel, which is here just visible through the graceful arch of an overbridge. A Garsdale-Hellifield local approaches behind. Stanier two-cylinder 2-6-4T No. 42648 on a June Saturday in 1958.

A Hellifield-Carlisle goods train leaving the northern end of Ribblehead Viaduct hauled by Class 8F 2-8 No. 48758. The faint outline of Pen-y-Ghent (2,273′) can be seen on the left.

An unidentified 9F 2-10-0 climbs away from Ribblehead Viaduct towards Blea Moor with empty wagons for Long Meg mine on 19 August 1967. Dominating the background is the massive bulk of Ingleborough.

Ribblehead station, looking south on a misty September day in 1963, with Stanier 'Black Five' No. 45275 running light towards the north. The style of architecture seen here is typical of the line, although the ornateness varies from station to station. Ribblehead has an austere appearance, in keeping with the high wild country which surrounds it.

Labouring up the gradient from Settle in June 1959 Fowler Class 4F No. 43902 passes the signal box at Stainforth Sidings on a northbound goods. The sidings, formerly serving the Craven Lime Company, no longer exist. To the left of the signal box, the white limestone walls typify the landscape around Settle.

The 4.40 p.m. Garsdale-Hellifield local heads south towards Settle through the rock cutting near Langcl in June 1957, behind Class 4MT 2-6-4 tank No. 42484. In the distance the limestone face of Winskill S dominates the scene.

British Railways' last official steam hauled train at speed near Long Preston on 11 August 1968, four years after the photograph opposite was taken at the same location. The locomotive, Britannia Class 7 4-6-2 No.70013 *Oliver Cromwell*, is now preserved at the Bressingham Museum.

Carlisle (Kingmoor) Class 5, No. 44901, swings through the curve near Long Preston and under the bridge carrying the road from Gisburn to Settle with the 3.40 p.m. Bradford (Forster Square)-Carlisle passenger in on a May day in 1964.

The down 'Thames-Clyde Express' approaching Hellifield in June 1957, headed by 'Royal Scot' No. 46145 *The Duke of Wellington's Regiment (West Riding)*.

The northbound 'Waverley' about to depart from Hellifield on a September afternoon in 1958 with 'Black Five' No. 44853 heading the train and Compound 4-4-0 No. 41119 as pilot.

Fowler Class 4F No. 44094 trundling south near Hellifield with an up freight in 1957.

'Royal Scot' class No. 46109 *Royal Engineer* forging ahead with the down
'Thames-Clyde Express' on the rising gradient towards Hellifield on
Whit Monday 1958.

Although photographed as late as 1957, this three-cylinder Compound 4-4-0 (No. 41186) with its Morecambe to Leeds passenger train has an attractively vintage look about it.

With spring flowers blooming in the meadows alongside the line, 'Jubilee' Class No. 45566 *Queensland* takes its train northward on its way from Leeds to Morecambe in 1958.

eds (Holbeck) 'Royal Scot' No. 46112 *Sherwood Forester* climbing northwards at the head of the down 'averley' in May 1958. Here the line passes alternately over embankments and through cuttings in order to aintain a consistent gradient as it traverses the undulating terrain between Skipton and Hellifield.

Three-cylinder Compound No. 41193 displaying a smart turn of speed as it races down the grade towards Skipton with a Morecambe-Leeds passenger train.

lodding along the embankment near Bell Busk, between Skipton and Hellifield, Class 4F 0-6-0 No.43913 ts a heavy rake of coal wagons northwards in May 1959.

Towards the end of a long and useful life Compound 4-4-0 No.41101 appears to be making light work of the gradient on a Leeds-Morecambe working near Bell Busk on a May evening in 1959.

Compared with the northern part of the line from Settle Junction to Carlisle, the southern end is busy with passenger traffic travelling between the Yorkshire cities of Leeds and Bradford and the Lancashire coast, Carnforth and the Lake District. Here Ivatt Class 4 2-6-0 No. 43108 coasts through the unspoilt countryside around Bell Busk heading a train for Leeds and Bradford.

A hard-working Fowler Class 4F, No. 44510, puts up a smoke screen as it heads a south-bound goods near Hellifield on a sunny day in June 1957.

Class 4F No.44216 with a rake of excursion stock approaching Bell Busk *en route* to Leeds in 1959, an unusual
task for this class of locomotive which was normally employed on freight duties.

'Jubilee' No. 45564 *New South Wales* sweeps through the curve as it leaves Bell Bu
cutting with the 12.43 p.m. Bradford (Forster Square) to Morecambe passenger train
May 1959.

Ivatt 'Mogul' Class 4 No. 43030 heading north from Bell Busk with a Leeds-Morecambe excursion in May 1959. This single chimney locomotive was one of the class originally built with double chimneys.

e Hughes/Fowler 2-6-0 locomotives, known as 'Crabs', were not normally employed on passenger traffic ween Skipton and Carlisle, but here No. 42751 is seen on passenger duty heading a Skipton-Morecambe ursion in Bell Busk cutting on Easter Saturday in 1960.

The 2.43 p.m. Carnforth-Leeds express passing Bell Busk station headed by Stanier 'Black Five' No. 44780. The station was closed to all traffic on 4 May 1959, three weeks before this photograph was taken.

An illustrious visitor to the line was former LNER Class 'A3' Pacific No. 4472 *Flying Scotsman*, here seen heading north past Bell Busk signal box on an enthusiasts' special organised by the Gainsborough Model Railway Society in May 1965.

One of the sturdy-looking Class 4F 0-6-0s which were commonly seen on heavy freight duties on the line, No. 44222 hauling a long rake of coal wagons northwards near Bell Busk.

Stanier Class 4MT 2-6-4 tank No. 42484 passing over the small viaduct which spans the River Aire, near Bank Newton, south of Bell Busk with a Bradford-Garsdale local in 1957. Close by, the river, canal and railway converge, necessitating interesting engineering works consisting of an aqueduct over the River Aire and a railway bridge over the aqueduct.

A Morecambe-
Bradford train swings
smartly through the
curve and under an
occupation bridge
near Bank Newton
headed by 'Crab'
2-6-0 No. 42702 in early
August of 1960.

The ubiquitous Class
4F represented by
No. 43913 fills the air
with sound and smoke
as it climbs towards
the highest of the three
levels of railway, canal
and river in the Aire
Valley north of
Gargrave in June 1957.

A Stanier Class 8F coasts down the grade towards Skipton with an up goods in August 1965.

The last of the 'Ro[y] Scots' to remain in service, No. 46115 *Scots Guardsman,* relegated to stoppi[ng] train duties, on a Bradford-Carlisle passenger working near Gargrave in J[une] 1965. *Scots Guardsr[nan]* is now preserved b[y] the Bahamas Locomotive Societ[y] at Dinting.

Stanier Class 5 No. 44756, fitted with Caprotti valve gear, appears to be approaching with arms akimbo at the head of a down parcels train near Gargrave in June 1963.

Ivatt Class 2 2-6-0 No. 46422 has a clear road ahead as it propels an inspector's saloon northward near Gargrave in 1962.

One of the few remaining members of the 'Patriot' Class locomotives still in service, No. 45543 *Home Guard* in charge
a Leeds-Morecambe train near Gargrave in June 1962. *Below:* W. D. Austerity 2-8-0 No. 90415 plodding steadily up
grade with a coke train between Skipton and Hellifield. So sedate was the pace that driver, fireman and photograph
were able to exchange leisurely greetings.

Stanier Class 5 4-6-0 No. 45148 threads its way through the clutter of the approaches at the eastern end of Skipton Station in 1963 with a train from Bradford to Carlisle.

Gargrave station echoes to the sound of No. 45711 *Courageous* speeding towards Skipton with an up express on a sunny September day in 1959.

'ubilee' Class No. 45592 *Indore* clears Gargrave Station with a Leeds to Morecambe and Carnforth express May 1961. After the advent of the large diesels on the long distance expresses, 'Jubilees' and 'Black ves' shared most of the local passenger traffic until their demise.

About two miles out of Skipton a northbound parcels train passes the crossing keeper's cottage with 'Crab' 2-6-0 No. 42895 in charge. Here the line lies between the Leeds and Liverpool Canal and the A59 road from Skipton to Preston.

nier 'Black Five' No. 44892 approaching the station at Gargrave at a leisurely pace
n a Leeds-Morecambe train in 1959.

A down goods train hauled by Class '5' No. 44912 approaches Skipton Station from the east, taking the route between the Colne and Ilkley platforms. The up and down main lines are on the extreme left whilst in the the background, to the left of the train, can be seen the original Skipton station building, erected in 1848 and demolished in 1967. The present station here was begun in 1875.

Skipton station, one of the celebrated Stanier 'Black Five' 4-6-0s, No. 45228, starts the 8 p.m. Carnforth-Leeds City train on 12th September 1963.

The 5.10 p.m. local passenger train for Preston, via Colne, waits to depart from Platform 4 at Skipton with one of the Skipton-based Ivatt Class 2MT 2-6-2 tanks at the head on 10 September 1958. The former Midland line from Colne joined the Skipton-Carlisle line about three-quarters of a mile west of Skipton station, but this link between Lancashire and Yorkshire was closed and the track lifted in 1970.